MELTON CONSTA
BRISTON AND DISTRICT

A Portrait in Old Picture Postcards

by

Rhoda Bunn

S. B. Publications
1991

This little book is dedicated to David who made the journey with me to this my favourite corner of Norfolk so often and to all friends in the area, old and new.

By the same author: *Holt and District.*

First published in 1991 by S.B. Publications.
Unit 2, The Old Station Yard, Pipe Gate, Nr. Market Drayton, Shropshire, TF9 4HY.

Typeset and printed by Geo. R. Reeve Ltd., Wymondham, Norfolk NR18 0BD.

CONTENTS

CONTENTS CONTINUED

CONTENTS CONTINUED

INTRODUCTION

Before the advent of the railways, Melton Constable was a tiny village of 19 houses and 100 people, most employed by Lord Hastings on his Estate. Farm labourers' wages were 16/- a week, so the Railway Company offered 18/- a week for labourers to construct the railroad. By the end of the century, a thriving community of 400 people had sprung up, increasing yearly as the line was extended, until in its heyday Melton's population was well over a thousand.

The story of the Work's closure and the demise of the M&GN is well known and in the space of 90 years, Melton's railway had come and gone, but it left behind a love of the old-fashioned steam engines that will always be remembered.

The M&GN – known as the "Muddle and Get Nowhere" – is called the "Missed and Greatly Needed" now.

Briston, once called Bureston, as one of the sources of the river Bure rises here, is a large and rambling "free" parish having no principal landowner or Lord of the Manor. Consequently it is recorded that all manner of dissenters, rogues, paupers and wild people settled here! Between 1840 and 1850 the parish sent 150 paupers to Canada to settle. Besides the church there were 4 chapels in the village – the Independent Methodist Chapel was blown down in a gale on March 4th, 1895.

Briston and Hindolvestone were largely agricultural villages until the coming of the railways to Melton Constable, when many of the men in the surrounding area found employment with the railway company.

I hope these postcards of times gone by depicting Melton Constable, Briston, other villages in the area and some of the people who lived there will bring back pleasant memories to older readers, and give an insight into the way things used to be to the younger generation.

Rhoda M. Bunn
Market Street
Wymondham

BURGH PARVA'S CHURCH AND RUINS, c. 1934

Burgh Parva is a tiny parish forming part of the civil parish of Melton Constable. The ancient church of St. Mary has been in ruins since Cromwellian times. The "Temporary" Church, made of corrugated iron, and affectionately known as the Tin Church, was erected early this century. The register dates from 1557. The vicar of Briston, at this time the Rev. Charles Woode, took services here also.

S 1359   THE STATION MELTON CONSTABLE.

MELTON CONSTABLE STATION, p.u. 1915

The First Class and Ladies' Waiting Room are shown in the right foreground, while W.H. Smith's Bookstall and the station approach railings are seen centre picture under the canopy. The bridge carries the road to Hindolvestone and Thursford. The tall building right of the bridge is the station entrance, with its flight of stone steps leading down to the ticket office and platforms. The tree on the left conceals Lord Hastings' private waiting room. Part of the Melton West signal-box is in view under the bridge.

MELTON CONSTABLE STATION, c. 1935

Looking east, this scene shows a goods train facing towards Norwich. The platform stretches as far as Melton East signal-box, centre background. To the left, the Company's gas works chimney can be seen with the coal and goods yards on the left out of view. Stock wagons and coal trucks stand in the right foreground.

RAILWAY REFRESHMENT ROOMS, c. 1915

In 1883, Henry Codling, licensee of the Hastings Arms became the first proprietor of the Railway Refreshment Rooms, but by 1900 the M&GN had taken over the management. The two fashionably dressed young ladies seen here are Alice Morgan and May Fields, who worked in the refreshment rooms. When the crowded excursion trains came into the station a large tea trolley was taken along the platform to serve drinks to the passengers. The Third Class Waiting Room entrance is on the right. Separate Ladies and First Class Waiting Rooms were also provided.

LORD HASTINGS' WAITING ROOM, c. 1935

This waiting room was built for the exclusive use of Lord Hastings, his family and guests when the station was built. Situated on the opposite side of the rails to the passenger platforms, it had its own private entrance on the Hindolvestone Road. It is believed that there was once an underground passage running under the track to the Refreshment Rooms opposite, so the staff could easily provide his Lordship's guests with any refreshments required. The engine turntable was situated just off the picture to the left.

MELTON STATION PORTERS, c. 1910

These young men, dressed in M&GN Porters' uniforms of the time, displayed the company's name on their caps, and initials on their waistcoat buttons. Flower buttonholes and well polished shoes completed their smart appearance. The porter on the left is known to be Dick Fisher. He was later promoted to Guard and served the company until retirement. Three of his five sons, Dick, Fred and Stanley also spent their working lives with the Railway.

CLEARING THE SNOW, c. 1927

M&GN staff disposing of snow after a heavy fall by shovelling it into wagons to be taken away by train. The signal-box in the right background is Melton West with the Fakenham and Lynn line to its left. The train is on the Holt and Cromer line. Belle Vue Tower is just visible on the right skyline.

S 1353   FITTING SHOP RAILWAY WORKS MELTON CONSTABLE

THE FITTING SHOP, MELTON WORKS, c. 1910

The size of the Fitting Shop, one of the many different departments at the Works, can be judged if compared with the engine in the foreground stripped down for repair. This engine, 0-6-0T no. 96, was one of 16 engines actually built at Melton, but many others were repaired and overhauled here over the years.

RELIGIOUS SERVICE, MELTON WORKS, c. 1914

Many troops were stationed in the area during the early days of the first world war. As the local church was far too small to accommodate such large gatherings for religious services, the Carriage Shop at Melton Works became the venue for the 5th Battalion Essex Regiment's Sunday Service on December 13, 1914. Music for the hymns was played on the harmonium seen on the right near the minister conducting the service.

THE LAST PASSENGER TRAIN, 1964

The last passenger train, a British Railway's Diesel, arrived at Melton Constable Station from Sheringham at 11.04 p.m. on April 4th, 1964; a sad time indeed for the local community. Pictured on the train are driver Ernie Stapleton and Mr. Harold Drewery, the stationmaster. On the platform are Mrs. S. Kirk, Mrs. Colman, Mrs. Harper and Mrs. G. Eke. The guard for the journey was Mr. Robert Jones.

(Picture courtesy Eastern Daily Press)

END OF THE LINE, c. 1971

Lord Hastings, the principal landowner in the area, provided about 11 acres of land for the building of the station and works; the first bricks laid on 10th May, 1881. Demolition of the station buildings, to make way for an automatic telephone exchange was undertaken by Mr. Sid Lubbock, the Briston builder, whose father had worked at the station before the first world war. Work commenced in April 1971, almost exactly ninety years after the station came into being. In this sad scene, the pile of rubble on the right is all that is left of W.H. Smith's bookstall, the platform roofing has gone and the waiting rooms were soon to follow.

(Picture courtesy of Eastern Daily Press)

"LEAVING-OFF" TIME, MELTON WORKS, c. 1914

This rare picture shows Melton Works' employees going home from work at 5.30 p.m. (indicated by long shadows). In the cente background, the road turned sharp left, with the works entrance in the Hindolvestone Road, just beyond the entrance to the station. The sharp corner was eliminated when the road was improved after the station was demolished in 1971. The Hastings Arms can be seen on the right.

MR. S. WRIGHT, GREENGROCER, c. 1937

Siddie Wright from Briston poses with his greengrocery cart drawn by his horse 'Nobby'. His shop was near Briston Green, previously kept by Mrs. Coble as a sweet shop. In the background, situated at the top of Melton Hill is George Ekes' hair-dressing salon where all the world's troubles were put right. George would always say: "Come in, you're next"; no matter how many customers were waiting! In the "Ladies End" off the picture, a "perm" would cost: ends – half a crown (12½p) or a whole head – five shillings (25p).

COLMAN'S GARAGE, c. 1932

Mr. Colman established a cycle and motor-cycle repair business in 1912. Later the business developed into a garage and filling station, and among the many services he provided was the recharging of accumulator batteries for wirelesses. Mr. Colman is shown above near the right-hand petrol pump; these hand-operated pumps are now at Caister Hall Museum.

S 5587   RECREATION GROUND, MELTON CONSTABLE

THE RECREATION GROUND, p.u. 1910

Showing the Bowling Green with a game in progress and the tennis court to the rear. The greenhouse in the gardens can be seen among the trees. Flowers grown here were sent along the line daily to decorate the vaious station waiting rooms. The M&GN gas works built in 1899 can just be seen on the right of the picture. Until these became operational, there was no public lighting in the district.

HASTINGS ARMS, c. 1910

Bullard's the Norwich brewers supplied Melton's only public house – the Hastings Arms – run by Thomas Cheney at the time this superb animated picture was taken. The yard is full of carts left by farmers, who stabled their horses at the pub while they went by train to the cattle and corn markets in Norwich. On the forecourt is a baker's cart, the shafts well up in the air, denoting a very heavy load. The Hastings Arms was built by Lord Hastings in 1883.

MELTON'S FIRST SHOP, c. 1908

Mr. Arthur Colman built this grocery store in 1894. Cycles were repaired here by his son Cyril, and stored while their owners travelled by train. The shop was extended in 1912, and Cyril then moved to his own premises near the Hastings Arms. Pictured left to right are: Mr. Hammond (later to become the Co-op manager), Cyril Colman, Sam Clarke, Reggie Colman, Mr. Codling, and the owner, Arthur Colman.

MELTON CONSTABLE RAILWAY INSTITUTE, p.u. 1912

The Railway Institute was opened by the Company for the use of their employees in 1896 and later enlarged in 1912. It contained a large hall used for all kinds of entertainments and public meetings, coffee and dining rooms, reading and billiard rooms and a library of 1,500 books, which were increased to 3,000 by the mid-1920s. A.Q. Newman was the secretary and H. Ellwood was the caretaker at the time of this photograph. The adjoining building on the right of the picture was Mr. Arthur Colman's grocery store.

MELTON STREET, MELTON CONSTABLE, c. 1912

This view of Melton Street shows the school in the background. This street of houses was the first to be built (1882) by the Railway Company for its workers, and all houses were supplied with gas from the Railway gas works, and running water. The employees' rents and water charges were deducted from their wages, along with 4d a week for membership to the Institute. When they left the Company's employ or retired, they had to vacate their houses. The ladders seen in the foreground were for use in case of fire, and red-painted firebuckets hung nearby.

MELTON'S FIRST POST OFFICE, p.u. 1903

Not much is known about this Post Office, except that it was situated in Melton Street; the side road just past the railway Institute, coming from the station. It closed when the new post office opened in the Main Street. All the houses on this side of the Main Street were built by the Railway Company to house their employees. The distinctive railings which surrounded all railway property can be seen in the foreground.

THE SCHOOLS. MELTON CONSTABLE 9121.

THE SCHOOL, MELTON CONSTABLE, p.u. 1912

Taken from the corner where Gordon Road (right) joins the main street, this picture shows the Public Elementary School, built in 1896. The cost was funded jointly by Lord Hastings and the Railway Company. It was enlarged twice, in 1900 and 1906, to accommodate 320 children (mixed and infants). Alfred Harmer was headmaster and Miss Ellen Locke the infant's mistress at this time. The school closed in 1984.

GORDON ROAD, p.u. 1912

Gordon Road is one of three side roads in the village with privately-built houses, the others being Kitchener and Burgh Beck Road. This view, with the school's playground railings on the left, shows Mr. George Joice's butcher's shop and a terrace of neat bay-windowed houses, many occupied by railway staff. Notice the splendid old gas-lamp in the left foreground.

BRISTON ROAD, MELTON CONSTABLE.

MELTON'S MAIN STREET, c. 1915

The group of children across the street adds greatly to the charm of this picture. Miss Nellie Linder, well-known for her sharp tongue, was in charge of the Post Office, shown on the left on the corner with Gordon Road, with the Police House adjoining. The next property was Dr. Welch's Surgery, built in 1896. The entrance to Colville Road is opposite near the street lamp, and the baker's cart is standing outside Mr. Alfred Rose's bakery.

MELTON'S FIRST TAXI, c. 1911

This magnificent motor car, with Cyril Colman at the wheel, was made by Alldays & Onions, the Pneumatic Engineering Company, Great Western Works, Small Heath, Birmingham and was transported by rail to Melton Constable station when purchased by Mr. Arthur Colman, the grocer. It is shown above parked in the Main Street outside Dr. Welch's surgery and waiting to take the doctor (who could not drive) on his rounds to visit his patients.

COLVILLE ROAD, p.u. 1915

Another street of M&GN-built houses but with the addition of newly-planted trees. Railway wagons in the Goods Yard can be seen in the background. The Gas Works entrance was at the end of this road, along with the shed housing the fire pumps. Mr. Alfred Rose's bakery, run for many years by Mr. Gaskin, stood on the corner of Colville Road and Main Street.

THE CO-OP, MELTON CONSTABLE, p.u. 1914

The Co-op Society's grocery store stood on the corner with Kitchener Road, with a large hall above, was used for the meetings and functions associated with the Co-op and Labour Movement. Also, a dentist attended here every Thursday in a room above the shop. The houses on this side of the street were all privately built and many were rented by M&GN employees, but water and gas were not laid on, as they were only available in the M&GN-built houses; the tenants having to manage with oil lamps and water from the pump.

Briston Road, Melton Constable. (*Fisher's Series.*) J 2537.

BRISTON ROAD, MELTON CONSTABLE, p.u. 1917

Looking towards the station, the shop in the right foreground is Fisher's chemists, with Mr. Fisher in the doorway. Mr. Fisher eventually built a larger shop opposite; Mr. W.O. Fisher was affectionately known as "Chemical Bill". Adjoining is A.W. Cooter's general drapery store, which later became the Co-op drapery department. The wooden building, left foreground, was occupied by Pasks, tailors, who made livery for Lord Hastings' staff at the Hall. The foreground marks the point where Melton and Briston join.

Lord Hastings estate Melton Constable

MELTON CONSTABLE HALL, p.u. 1904

This elegant mansion built by Sir Jacob Astley in 1680 on the site of the previous Hall, stands in 800 acres of park and woodland. The Park itself, four miles in circumference is partly walled, and contained herds of red and fallow deer. It is one of the oldest enclosures in England and has belonged to the Astleys – the family name of Lord Hastings – for seven centuries. The Hall, which was empty for several years, was the location of the film "The Go-Between" and is at present undergoing extensive restoration.

BELLE VUE TOWER, BRININGHAM, c. 1930

Originally a smock mill built in 1721 by Sir Jacob Astley of Melton Constable Hall, and located on the highest mill site in Norfolk; Sir Edward Astley had the present tower built on the same site in the mid-1770s. It contained richly furnished apartments used to accommodate gentlemen invited to shooting parties. The gamekeeper lived in a wooden building beside the tower, and it was here that visitors' meals were cooked. Originally a lead statue of a man with a gun stood on top of the tower, but this melted during a fire in one of the upper rooms. Belle Vue (now a private dwelling) commands an extensive view of the countryside, even down to the sea, and it was used as a lookout for ships and poachers.

BELLE VUE TOWER, MELTON CONSTABLE. J 7527. (Co-op. Society's Series.)

THE CRAWFISH, THURSFORD, c. 1918

The "Crawfish", the only public house of this name in Norfolk, was kept for many years by Arthur Esgate, the gentleman in the fancy cap on the left of the group. His wife, Norah, is on the decorated float holding the horse's reins. The occasion is thought to be part of the Peace celebrations. Thursford, a mainly agricultural village with a population of 225 at the time, had a station on the M&GN's Melton Constable to Lynn Line. Mr. George Cushing's famous Fair Organ and Steam Engine Museum is situated here.

SWANTON NOVERS, p.u. 1908

The village of Swanton Novers is situated close to Melton Constable Park; Lord Hastings was Lord of the Manor and chief landowner here. Nearby, Swanton Great Wood was famous for its game, including woodcock, and for its lilies-of-the-valley. Permits priced at 1/- could be purchased for the holders to gather 4 bunches of lilies, with the proceeds given to local charities. Much of the soil here is brick-clay, and rough earthenware and bricks were made at the Brickworks on the Guist Road. It is recorded that Norwich Cathedral could be seen from the tower of St. Edmund's church.

Fulmodestone Shop & Street

FULMODESTON STREET, c. 1912

Thomas Henry Hawes kept this grocery and drapery shop since the mid-1890s. It is believed that the photograph shows Mr. Hawes and his wife in the doorway. Groceries were also sold at the Post Office, where John Emerson was postmaster at this time. Fulmodeston is united with Croxton forming one scattered parish, two miles from Thursford. St. Mary's church was closed in 1882 and Christchurch was built in the same year. There were 220 acres of woodland in the village, said to contain some of the finest fir and pine trees in the county, and belonging to the Earl of Leicester, who was Lord of the Manor, and to Lord Hastings.

GUIST CROSSROADS, p.u. 1919

This view was considerably altered by Sir Thomas Cook's improvements to the village in 1928–29. The clock tower now stands where the signpost is sited, the village hall was built at the rear of the green and a row of cottages stand along the Holt Road. The horse and cart is travelling along the main Norwich to Fakenham Road.

SENNOWE PARK FIRE BRIGADE, p.u. 1933

Guist's Fire Station was generously provided for the village by Sir Thomas Cook, in 1929. Pictured here are the Brigade, captained by W.J. Beck, with their fire-engine which was stationed at Sennowe Park.

Post Office. Guist

GUIST POST OFFICE, c. 1907

Guist's busy Post Office and grocery shop with postmaster Thomas Vincent standing in the doorway and several postmen grouped in front of a motor-van. When Sir Thomas Cook made the improvements to the village in 1928–29, he built a new Post Office, where Mr. Vincent continued as postmaster.

The School, Gt. Ryburgh

THE SCHOOL, GREAT RYBURGH, c. 1912

A charming study of a typical Victorian village school, in this case the Public Elementary School at Great Ryburgh.
Standing on a corner site in the village centre, it was built in 1872 and enlarged in 1902 to take 250 children. The Master
at the time was Mr. Albert Foster (possibly the gentleman standing in the centre) and Mrs. Foster was Mistress of the
Infants' School. Unlike many Norfolk village schools which have sadly closed, this one is still in use.

GREAT RYBURGH SCHOOL, c. 1912

The interior of the same school and showing the pupils sharing bench-desks, the teacher's desk and a piano. The glass partition could be pulled across to divide the room into two classes. The walls are decorated with various cases of stuffed animals, deerheads, crossed swords and shields and a large collection of books at the far end; a contrast to today's computerised education! In those days, the School would have been heated by open coal fires.

"The Malting's", Gt. Ryburgh.

STATION AND MALTINGS, GREAT RYBURGH, p.u. 1905

Great Ryburgh's station was on the Wymondham to Wells branch-line of the Great Eastern Railway. Situated beside the station is the huge Maltings complex owned by F. and G. Smith Ltd., maltsters, millers (steam and water) and general feed merchants. The company had been on the site previous to 1875 and also had premises at Wells Quay and at East Dereham. Smith's wagon loading on the foreground was pulled by two horses. Notice the small cart lamps for night driving. The Maltings are still operational and at the time of writing a modern industrial site called the New Maltings Development is being constructed.

BINTRY WATER MILL, p.u. 1913

Water mills were in existence before the arrival of the windmill in England in the 12th century. It is thought that the site of this mill at Bintry is very ancient. The mill was owned from the mid-1800s to the turn of the century by the Burrell family and then for a short time by Fred Sharpin, before Seaman & Sons became the owners. This postcard was produced by William Isaac Butler, a Bintry grocer.

WATTS NAVAL TRAINING SCHOOL, NORTH ELMHAM, NORFOLK.

WATTS NAVAL TRAINING SCHOOL, NORTH ELMHAM, p.u. 1904

Standing on top of a hill on a 54-acre site and constructed in the Domestic Gothic style, this building was originally Norfolk County School. The Foundation Stone was laid on Easter Monday 1873 by the Prince of Wales. The School opened in 1874 and closed in July 1895. It was re-established by E.H. Watts Esq. as a naval training school for orphan and destitute boys in the care of Dr. Barnardo in 1901. The building was demolished several years ago.

Watts' Naval Boys at Reepham Garden Fête Dr Perry's Grounds

WATTS NAVAL BOYS AT REEPHAM, c. 1910

The school, officially recognised by the Admiralty, accommodated 300 boys who trained for the Navy and Mercantile Marine. The boys from Watts Naval School were much in demand for entertaining at local functions. They are seen performing here at a garden fête held in Dr. Edward Perry's grounds at Reepham.

GOODS COLLISION AT GUESTWICK, 31.10.1908

The M&GN had remarkably few accidents, but occasionally one did occur. Pictured here is a derailment outside Guestwick Station; the station buildings shown on the left, near the signal. The no. 36 engine involved in the accident had its buffers damaged and was taken to Melton Works for repair. The Company's travelling crane is seen recovering a de-railed wagon under the watchful eye of Mr. William Marriott, M&GN's Engineer and Loomotive Superintendent (2nd from right).

JᴬS 5888   **Hindolvestone Church.**

HINDOLVESTONE CHURCH, c. 1905

Situated at the end of the village, St. George's church was built in the perpendicular style. One Sunday afternoon, 31st July, 1892, the church tower collapsed suddenly through the church roof. Two young boys, Alfred Brett and Herbert Fisher, who were playing nearby were the first to run to the vicarage with the devastating news. In January 1893, a temporary wooden building was licensed for divine services and used until the present church was built in 1932, using material from the old church. Herbert Fisher was the author's father.

CHURCH PARADE, c. 1919

Photographed outside the Chequers at the start of a church parade in August 1919, and showing members of the Hindolvestone Brass Band in their smart "frogged" uniforms, and some of the villagers. The band was founded in 1902. The Chequers public house closed eventually, along with the village's other pubs, and has now been converted into a private house.

HINDOLVESTONE POST OFFICE, p.u. 1906

The postmaster at this time was Orris William Pegg who was also a baker, grocer and draper. Letters were received through Dereham by foot-messenger from Guist on weekdays and Sundays. Postal orders were issued, but not paid here and the Telegaph Office was at the railway station; a complicated system. The paraffin delivery cart on the forecourt belonged to the Consolidated Petroleum Company, which sold Rock Light lamp oil to the shops. The post office is in the same building today.

4942 THE POST OFFICE, HINDOLVESTONE.

HINDOLVESTONE POST OFFICE, p.u. 1909

A delightful picture of the Post Office, now moved to premises on the opposite side of the road, with Mrs. Agnes Bowman as postmistress and proprietress of the bakery on right of picture. Some of her staff can be seen loading the delivery cart, outside the shop. These premises – the house, bakery, Hindolvestone's windmill and three cottages – were later sold together for £310 and the Post Office then reverted back to where it is today.

THE WINDMILL, HINDOLVESTONE, c. 1923

This 40ft.-high mill was built by John Pegg in 1844 to replace a post-mill owned by him which stood on the opposite side of the main street. In 1906 Mrs. Agnes Bowman operated the mill, having rented the adjacent bakery and shop as well. Mr. Harry Davison took over the business in 1922 and the mill continued working until the early 1930s. A new boat-shaped cap has been fitted and the mill has been converted to a private dwelling.

10,401   The Mill, Hindolvestone.   Davison's Series.

HINDOLVESTONE STATION, c. 1922

This neat little station was the first stop from Melton Constable, on the way to Norwich City station; the trains from City station arriving from the left of the picture. Notice the poster advertising "Furness Railway for the English Lakes", and two enamel Pears' soap advertisements on the wall. The two people on the left are believed to be Mr. F.G. Bateman, the stationmaster, and his wife.

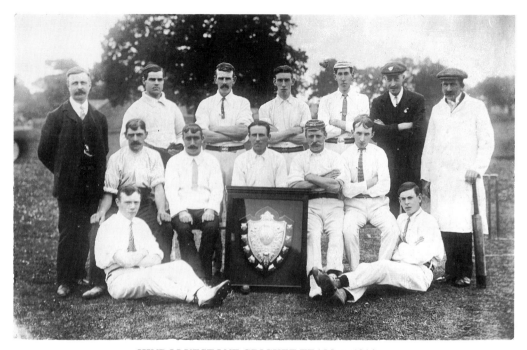

HINDOLVESTONE CRICKET TEAM, c. 1914

Having won the "Shield", the village's cricketers are pictured proudly displaying their trophy. Standing on the left is Mr. Frederick Bateman, Hindolvestone's stationmaster. On the back row (left to right) are: Herbert Fisher, Albert Strike, ? Reeve, Jimmy Cooper, Herbert Long and George Lockett (umpire). Seated on the ground are: Arthur Holsey (left) and George Cooper. After 76 years the names of the centre row are uncertain, but Walter Codling, Albert Bunkell and Laurence Eke are three names suggested. Can any reader identify the centre row?

THE STREET, HINDOLVESTONE, c. 1947

The building on the left was occupied by the old National School and used until the Board School was built in 1889, when it became the Church Mission Room. Later Mr. and Mrs. Leslie Wakefield opened it as a general store in 1947 and traded there for 29 years, closing in 1976. Mr. Wakefield was also a cycle agent, and kept a fish and chip shop (marked with a cross on this postcard). The premises of Mr. J. Parker and Sons, motor engineers, haulage contractors, bus proprietors and radio dealers can be seen on the opposite side of the street.

THE FLOODS AT THURNING, c. 1912

During the devastating floods which occurred on 26th August, 1912, the River Thurne became a torrent which completely washed away the brick bridge. It is believed that the three people in the picture are the Misses Ellen and Rose Gay and their brother James, who lived at Thurning Hall. The Gays owned all the land in Thurning except for one farm, with the River Thurne diverted to form a lake in the Hall grounds. One of their ancestors, also James Gay, wrote in the 1760s that he owed his "attainment to high office in Ceylon" to his education at Greshams School, Holt.

WATERMERE MILL, BRISTON, c. 1910

Once the scene of much activity, this old mill stands in water meadows by the Bridle Road leading from Craymere Beck. Situated on the boundary between Briston and Thurning, it stood forlorn and derelict for many years, but has recently been converted into a private house.

FISHING AT WATERMERE, BRISTON, c. 1910
The Fisherman's Prayer must have been answered for Mr. Jack Wheatley, shown here with a young companion, displaying a pike caught while fishing from a Norfolk punt, on the river near the mill. The tall reeds in the background complete a charming picture.

MR. BARWICK, TAXI DRIVER, BRISTON, c. 1930

After the first world war, Bertie Barwick started his taxi business using a horse and trap and a wagonette. As trade increased and the work became too much for the horses, he changed to motor-transport, always driving a Citroen car – renowned for comfort even in those days – as he had sustained severe leg injuries in the war. Mr. Barwick is shown above at the wheel of his first motor car. His passengers are Mrs. Jex, secretary to the Primitive Methodist Chapel, and her grandson Kenny. Mr. Barwick was also a Briston Parish Councillor, District Councillor and School Governor to the Primary School. Kenny Jex was also to become a Parish Councillor in later years.

HALL STREET, BRISTON, c. 1933

Shown in the left foreground is Jimmy Strutt's basket-maker's shop with the Primitive Methodist Chapel further down. The chapel was built in 1832 of stone from the Craymere Road Common, and enlarged in 1891 to hold 300 persons. The Chapel closed in July, 1969. Mrs. Barwick's general store can be seen beyond, in front of Jimmy Bangay's cottage. The cottages in the right foreground, under a Demolition Order since 1934, were finally taken down in 1955. The next house was occupied by Mr. Bertie Barwick. The road leads from the railway crossing to the village centre.

JIMMY STRUTT, c. 1937

Jimmy Strutt was a familiar figure pushing his handcart around Briston and Melton, led by his little dog, because Jimmy was blind. He had been trained as a basket-maker and also sold other items such as shoe laces. He always found his way in safety and is photographed here outside Rose's bakery in Melton Constable, one and a half miles from home. Jimmy's shop was situated in Hall Street, shown on page 55.

THE "GREEN MAN", BRISTON, p.u. 1906

At the time of this photograph, The Green Man was kept by Alfred Williams. He became landlord in the 1870s, before the railroad was laid through Briston. Beer was 2d a pint, and the popular games played at the pub were skittles, draughts and dominoes. Sometimes a wandering fiddler would call in to play a few tunes, and a raffle was always held at Christmas. Mr. Williams was landlord for over 50 years, retiring in the 1920s. The entrance to William Shingler's Nurseries is near the group of children, then the road curves right, in front of Devonshire House, towards the village centre. The Green Man is still open.

BRISTON'S FOOTBALL TEAM, c. 1946

Briston always had a strong football team, called the "Stars". Their home pitch was on the "Rec" in Hall Street, where a new Pavilion was built in the 1930s. Pictured left to right standing are:- Billy Lubbock, Arthur Hall, John Fisher, Jack Wiggins, David Scott, Jimmy Fisher, Bob Cushion. Front Row:- John Lubbock, Gerald George, Reggie Goldsmith and Jerry Taberham.

THE GRANGE, HALL STREET, c. 1905

Messrs. J. & T. Woodcock ran this thriving business which also sold all kinds of animal and poultry feed. By the 1920s Mr. Gresham Woodcock had taken over. He was also Postmaster, the village Post Office being just off the picture to the right, facing the seed rooms. Both are now demolished and only the Grange still stands.

MR. EGGLETON'S TRACTION ENGINE, BRISTON, c. 1927

James Eggleton, landlord of Briston's "Half Moon" is seen here outside the inn with his grandson, Sidney, on his newly acquired Burrell traction engine, used for contract work. When some of the family, including Sidney, went to fetch the engine, it took 2 days (2.30 Saturday to 2.30 Monday) to complete the journey home, as they stopped at every pub on the way.

"HALF MOON" QUOITS TEAM, c. 1927

Quoits was a game widely played in Norfolk at this time, mostly at pubs, which had quoit beds in their grounds. Pictured above are the team from Briston Half Moon; winners of the Thomas Cook cup for 1927. The match was played at Sennowe Park, Guist. Standing left to right the players were: Charlie Bligh, H. Fabb, Stand Barwick, Wilfred Eggleton and B. Yarham. Seated left to right are: Knights Eggleton, Sid Lubbock and Walter Yarham.

CHURCH STREET, BRISTON.

THE GREEN AND CHURCH STREET, BRISTON, p.u. 1907

The building covered with posters was Samuel Fowl's blacksmith's shop. It conceals the village Reading Room to the rear of the shop premises next door. All Saints Church is seen in the centre on the skyline. By the 1930s Mr. Dennis was blacksmith, Mrs. Coble kept the sweet shop and the house to the left of the men in the street had become Mr. Billy Godfrey's fish and chip shop where "Two Tuppenny and two" (2 portions of cod and 2 pennyworth of chips) for 6d (2½ pence) was a good meal for two people! By then the tree on the Green was full grown and the Salvation Army Band held their service here on Sundays. Mill Lane runs to the right and Hall Street to the left.

BRISTON FAIR, c. 1925

Many will recall the week-long fairs held on Briston Green, twice yearly, May and October. Kenny Gray's steam-horses, "Rhubarb" Underwood's cakewalk, swingboats, children's roundabouts, coconut shies, Mrs. Gizzi's home-made rock stall and Mr. Cannell's wonderful chip cart, with it's gleaming copper pans, all attended. The large crowds which gathered for the event are shown here. A sheep and cattle sale was also held on the last Thursday in May in conjunction with the fair.

THE CAVALRY AT BRISTON, c. 1915

Many units of cavalry were stationed in Norfolk during the first world war. The soldiers pictured here on Briston Green belonged to the Berkshire Yeomanry who were sent to France the same year. Hall Farm can be seen in the background, occupied then by Edmund Williamson.

"FOURSES" AT FROGMORE FARM, BRISTON, c. 1929

Fourses is the name for afternoon refreshment taken to the harvest field. This picture shows District Nurse Edith Goose pouring tea for Charlie Howe – a welcome break from the hot, dusty work of stacking. Farmer Alfred Williamson is on the ladder, his son Henry below him, son Herbert on the stack, and daughter Anna is handing the tea round.

BRISTON BRASS BAND, c. 1919

Briston had its own brass band, pictured here outside the village Reading Room in Church Street, and before assembling to lead the Peace Parade. The band attended many functions including sports events, garden parties, flower shows and parades, both in Briston and the villages around. Several of the bandsmen worked for the M&GN at Melton. Mr. Miller (third left, front row) and H. Fisher (third left, back row) among them.

All Saints' Church, Briston. (*Fisher's Series.*) J 1860.

ALL SAINTS CHURCH, BRISTON, c. 1917

Standing in the village centre, All Saints Church was built in the Decorated and Perpendicular styles. It once had a round tower which became so unsafe it was taken down in 1785 and was replaced by a small turret containing one bell. There is seating for 250 people, and the register dates from 1689.

BRISTON'S LARGEST SHOP, p.u. 26.10.13

Owned by Mr. George Webber, who was a grocer, draper, hatter, hosier, general outfitter and also published his own post-cards, this shop stood in Church Street and was called Waterloo House. The living accommodation is on the left, with the churchyard wall beyond. The centre part of the shop, which became derelict, has been pulled down now.

CHEQUERS INN, BRISTON, c. 1928

The Chequers Inn in Church Street was one of Briston's five public houses. The landlord from 1920–45 was Mr. Sidney Hewitt who had taken over the tenancy from his father, George Hewitt. The bars and tap room are on the right, living quarters in the centre, and left the upper-storey club room used for various meetings and functions including weekly dancing classes, held by sisters Beryl and Trixie Phillips; the music supplied by a wind-up gramophone! Mrs. Eva Hewitt, the landlord's wife, is seen outside with daughter Rene and friend, Hetty Barsted.

PEACE CELEBRATIONS, BRISTON, 19th July, 1919

Among the centre group gathered for the parade outside the Chequers Inn is believed to be Mrs. Sands, her son Hubert right, and Fred Cork to the left of her. George Wheatley stands on the extreme left, and the Rev. Wooster with his cycle looks on. Herbert Stroulger's bakery stands in the centre background, and the front room of the house in Aubrey Terrace with the "Bank" sign over the door was occupied by Barclays Bank and opened on Fridays only, between 10 and 12 o'clock.

POST OFFICE CORNER, BRISTON, c. 1934

The corner of the post office and general stores run by brothers Stanley and Albert Howe can be seen on the extreme left with Oddfellows Hall nearby; both buildings have now been demolished with new housing built on the site. Garrood's bakery is on the right, and "The Manse" facing centre background. Notice the Eldorado ice cream pedal vehicle, a once familiar sight, ridden on this occasion by Willy Perry. Mr. Clitheroe from Edgefield is believed to be the driver of the horse and cart.

BRISTON FLOWER SHOW, c. 1922

This was a popular annual event held on the meadow behind Mr. George Hewitt's home, Norfolk House. The committee pictured here with some of the villagers are: (left to right) the Rev. Wooster, Dr. Welsh, Arthur Roe (grocer and draper), Mr. Roberts, George Hewitt (coal merchant), Jack Carter (Crossways Farm), and Mr. Perry (School master, Melton Road). The little girl, finger in mouth, is Muriel Eggleton, who lived at the Half Moon Inn.

ODDFELLOWS HALL, c. 1926

Mr. Harvey photographed after his final touches to the paintwork, before the official opening of the Hall. Every village function, from whist-drives to wedding receptions were held here, also a cinema two nights per week, beginning with silent films. The first colour film shown in the mid-1930s was "Gods Country and the Woman" starring Sylvia Sidney, with balloons given to the local children to mark the occasion. The Hall was recently demolished to make way for housing.

1st BRISTON GIRL GUIDES, 1st July, 1937

For a few years during the 1930s Briston had its own troop of girl guides. Pictured here standing left to right are: Alice Whittred, Jean Stimpson, Violet Oswick, Ruby Golden, Irene Hewitt, Captain B. Allen, Muriel Newman, Doris Bunkell, Janet Mears, Kathleen Carr, Joan Graveling. Sitting left to right are: Rhoda Fisher, Margaret Cushing, Elsie Le Grys, Helen Cushing, Gwenneth Matthew and Muriel Perry. Everyone remembered!

Stody Woods, Melton Constable.

STODY WOODS, c. 1916

Stody Woods – pictured here at the Briston crossroads – was nice and cool in the summer time, and always a popular venue for Sunday afternoon walks. Notice the local lads congregated round the large trees on the left; one of their favourite pastimes was to carve their intials on the tree trunk.

In the Matter of the Inclosure of the Common,

SITUATE IN THE PARISH OF

BRISTON, IN THE COUNTY OF NORFOLK.

PARTICULARS AND CONDITIONS OF SALE,

OF VALUABLE

FREEHOLD AND TITHE FREE

BUILDING, GARDEN,

OR

ACCOMMODATION LANDS,

Forming part of the Commons or Waste Grounds,

IN THE ABOVE PARISH,

TO BE SOLD BY AUCTION,

IN SIXTEEN LOTS,

BY

MESSRS. IRELAND,

ON

Tuesday, the 14th Day of July, 1868,

AT THE "HALF-MOON INN," BRISTON,

AT THREE O'CLOCK IN THE AFTERNOON,

By direction of Mr. Charles Horne, the Valuer acting in this matter, and with the approbation of The Inclosure Commissioners for England and Wales.

Particulars and Conditions of Sale, with Lithographed Maps, may be had of Mr. Charles Horne, Norwich, and of the Auctioneers, Wood Dalling, Guestwick, and Norwich.

GLOSCUP AND SON, PRINTERS, MARKET-PLACE, AYLSHAM.

BRISTON'S COMMON LAND SALE, c. 1868

Reduced to postcard size and showing the original poster advertising the sale of commons lands under the 1810 Enclosure Act. In all, nearly 50 acres of land were sold that day, in 16 lots of varying size, in different parts of the village: The Craymere, Reepham Road, Mill Lane and Edgefield areas.

BRISTON, WEST END.

EDGEFIELD ROAD, BRISTON, c. 1908

Facing east, this road passes through the West End and bears left towards Edgefield. The six pairs of houses (left) were built in the late 1800s on part of Horseshoes Common – sold in the 1868 Enclosure Sale (see previous page). The site, sold as Lots 1 and 2, was bought by Henry Barnard Beane, a farmer from Great Snoring. James Plumb, Clarence House, bought the houses in 1900. New houses built since the second world war now occupy the opposite side of the road.

West End, Briston, Melton Constable.

WEST END, BRISTON, c. 1916

The West End was a self contained little community, with two shops and the Horseshoes Inn nearby. Mr. Fisher sold groceries, sweets and perfume, and toys at Christmas in the shop shown above. He later moved to Melton Constable. Among the group of children are: Ernie Duffield sitting on the window sill, Lolly Sewell in the white jumper (right), and the four Fisher brothers (centre) grouped round the dog. Briston vicarage, then occupied by the Rev. Wooster, is shown in the background at the end of Edgefield Road.

PEASE'S BAKERY, MELTON ROAD, p.u. 1914

Facing towards Melton Constable, this scene shows Mr. Abraham David Pease's bakery in the foreground. Notice the bread delivery hand-cart outside. The business later became Bushell's bakery. Manor farmhouse and buildings can be seen in the background and the scene remains much the same today, except for the bakery which is no longer there.

ATTOE AND TWIDDY'S COAL CART, c. 1920

Having loaded the cart from their depot at Melton Station, Messrs. Attoe (seated) and Twiddy (standing), Briston coal merchants, are shown on their way to Briston to make deliveries; a hard and dirty day's work. They are pictured near the point where Melton joins Briston.

ACKNOWLEDGEMENTS

My grateful thanks are due to Mrs. Sibyl Kirk for access to her notes on Melton Constable and for all her other assistance, Molly and Dick Barwick, Mrs. Alice Jeary, Mrs. Rene Mendham and Miss Anna Williamson for their kindness in helping with facts and information, and to my daughters Chris and Jane for typing.

For the loan of postcards:-

Molly and Dick Barwick, pages 54 and 55.
Alice Jeary, page 58.
Rene Mendham, page 69.

Abbreviations used in text: c. - circa; p.u. - postally used.

Many of the Melton Constable street views were published by Coens of Norwich, others by Jarrolds of Norwich, the Co-op Society, Fishers Stores, and by W.H. Smith & Son. Herbert Remington, the Briston photographer, published many of the postcards of events, groups, etc. in that village.

Local titles published by S.B. Publications in the series: "A Portrait in Old Picture Postcards".

Huntingdonshire, Vols. 1 & 2
Peterborough, Vols. 1, 2 & 3
The Villages of Old Cambridgeshire
Wicken, a fen village

Hertfordshire, Vols. 1, 2 & 3

From Highgate to Hornsey
The Parish of St. Mary, Islington

Seaford & District
Eastbourne, Vol. 1

Great Yarmouth, Vol. 1
Holt & District
Norwich, Vols. 1, 2 & 3
The Norfolk Broads
Thetford, Brandon & District
West Norfolk
Norfolk's Railways, Vol. 1 - G.E.R.
Beccles and Bungay
East Suffolk

Newcastle-upon-Tyne, Vol. 1
Newcastle United

Other titles available and in preparation. For details write to S.B. Publications (enclosing S.A.E.) to:-
Unit 2, The Old Station Yard, Pipe Gate, Market Drayton, Shropshire, TF9 4HY.